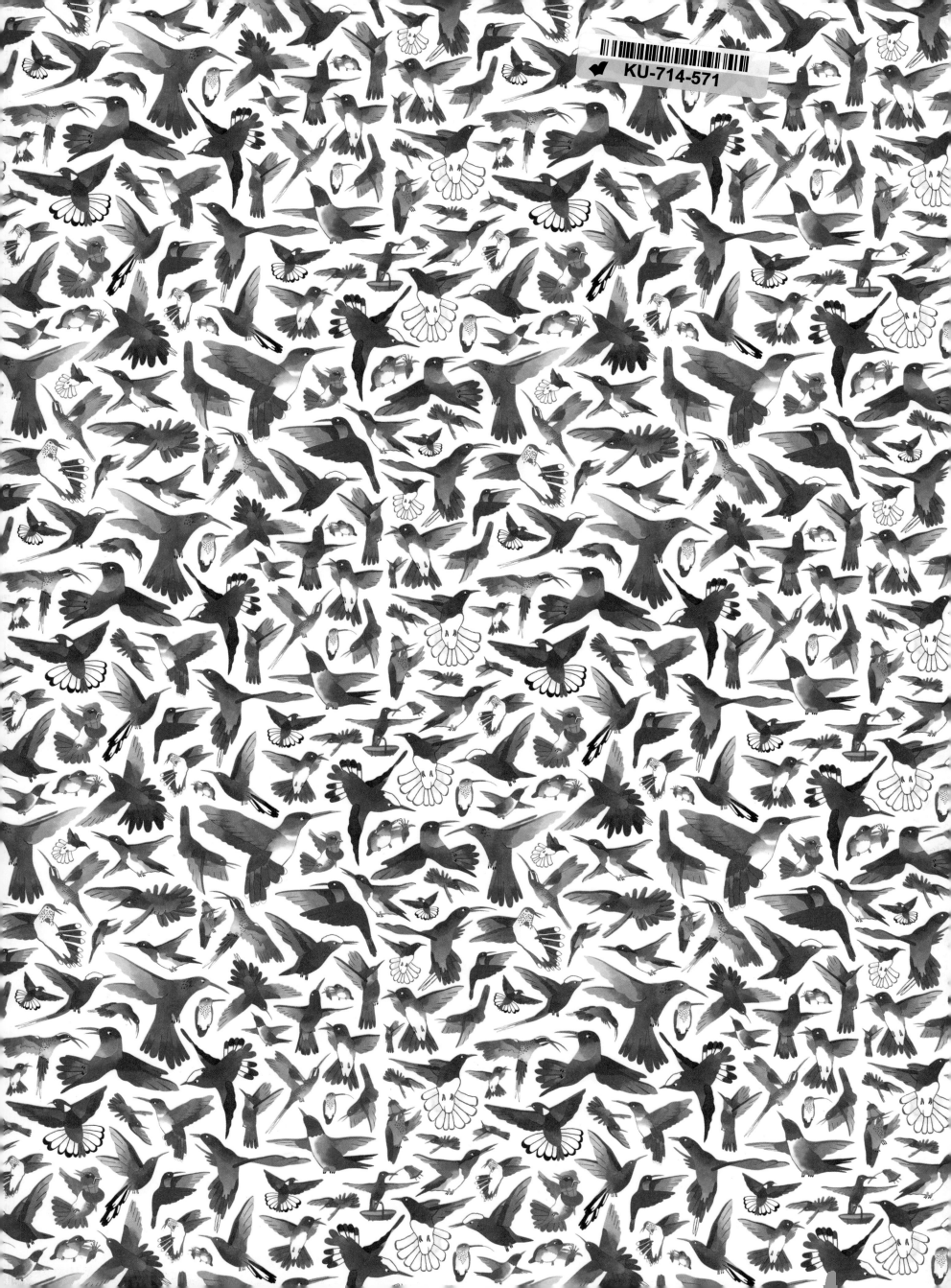

ATLAS OF ANIMAL ADVENTURES

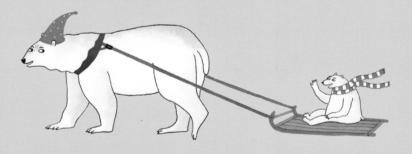

WIDE EYED EDITIONS

North
America

Central
America

South
America

Africa

WORLD
MAP

Europe

Asia

Middle East

Australasia & Oceania

Antarctica

N
W   E
S

CONTENTS

EMBARK ON AN ADVEN

Wildebeest

Fruit Bat

Hippopotamus

Sardine

Green Sea Turtle

Polar Bear

Puffin

Honeybee

Barn Owl

Siberian Tiger

Giant Panda

Orang-utan

Bird of Paradise

Bowerbird

Platypus

Red Kangaroo

Sockeye Salmon

Narwhal

Caribou

Black Bear

Peacock

Hummingbird

Humpback Whale

Sea Lion

Emperor Penguin

This book celebrates the incredible ways in which animals survive in the wild. With every turn of the page, you'll meet some of nature's most adventurous creatures, learning about their amazing behaviours and their epic migrations to the four corners of the Earth.

Look in detail at the animal in the spotlight of every scene. What new things will you learn about them and the habitats they call home?

Get to know each creature and understand its unique place in our world. Which animal will you adventure with today?

Asian Elephant

Iguana

Leaf-cutter Ant

Green Anaconda

Arctic Tern

Weddell Seal

AFRICA

Africa is home to some of the world's most headline-grabbing wildlife acts, from lions and leopards to elephants, rhinos and giraffes. This continent's wide savannahs, dense jungles and rich oceans are teeming with creatures, each with their own incredible survival secrets.

Monkeying around with the BARBARY MACAQUES (Morocco)

Madeira

Canary Islands

Morocco

Trekking with the CAMELS (Algeria)

Western Sahara

Mauritania

Taking wing with the PAINTED LADIES (Mauritania)

Mali

Cape Verde

Senegal

The Gambia

Guinea-Bissau

Guinea

Burkina Faso

Sierra Leone

Ivory Coast

Ghana

Liberia

Togo

North Atlantic Ocean

Ascension Island

St Helena

South Atlantic Ocean

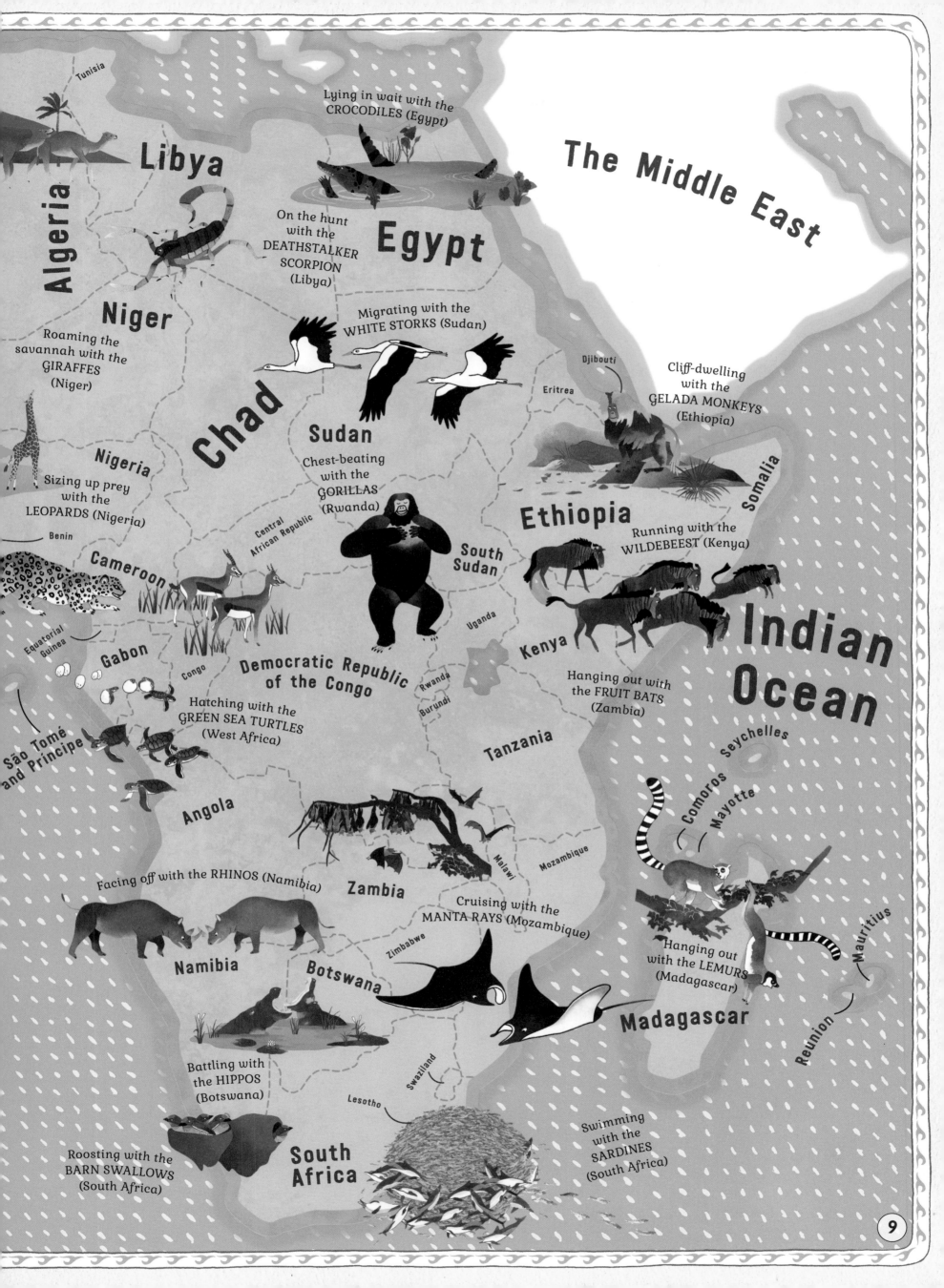

Tunisia

Libya

Algeria

Lying in wait with the
CROCODILES (Egypt)

The Middle East

On the hunt
with the
DEATHSTALKER
SCORPION
(Libya)

Egypt

Niger

Roaming the
savannah with the
GIRAFFES
(Niger)

Migrating with the
WHITE STORKS (Sudan)

Djibouti

Cliff-dwelling
with the
GELADA MONKEYS
(Ethiopia)

Eritrea

Chad

Sudan

Nigeria

Sizing up prey
with the
LEOPARDS (Nigeria)

Chest-beating
with the
GORILLAS
(Rwanda)

Central
African Republic

South
Sudan

Ethiopia

Somalia

Benin

Cameroon

Running with the
WILDEBEEST (Kenya)

Equatorial
Guinea

Gabon

Congo

Uganda

Kenya

Indian

São Tomé
and Príncipe

Hatching with the
GREEN SEA TURTLES
(West Africa)

Democratic Republic
of the Congo

Rwanda

Burundi

Hanging out with
the FRUIT BATS
(Zambia)

Ocean

Tanzania

Comoros

Seychelles

Mayotte

Angola

Malawi

Mozambique

Facing off with the RHINOS (Namibia)

Zambia

Cruising with the
MANTA RAYS (Mozambique)

Hanging out
with the LEMURS
(Madagascar)

Namibia

Botswana

Zimbabwe

Mauritius

Battling with
the HIPPOS
(Botswana)

Swaziland

Madagascar

Réunion

Lesotho

Swimming
with the
SARDINES
(South Africa)

Roosting with the
BARN SWALLOWS
(South Africa)

South
Africa

9

KENYA

Wildebeest migration

TANZANIA

Wildebeest herds can travel up to 3,000 kilometres each year in search of water and fresh grass to eat.

Hungry vultures circle the river, waiting to pick through the remains of any creatures that don't survive the crossing.

When zebras are in a herd, their stripes merge together and make it difficult for hunters to single out a particular animal.

Wildebeest can run at speeds of up to 80 kilometres per hour, and may inflict serious damage on any animals in their way!

By the time they reach the river, the animals are often weak after their long journey, but they need to keep their wits about them because danger is everywhere.

Curved horns for defence

Stripes break up outline to make wildebeest harder to see

Long, bushy tail to flick flies away

Distinctive black mane and beard of hair beneath chin

The wildebeest of East Africa have undertaken this world-famous migration for thousands of years.

Over a million wildebeest attempt this journey every year, along with 350,000 gazelles and 200,000 zebras.

Lions crouch in hiding, ready to pounce on the stragglers as they emerge from the water.

The Mara River is home to some of the largest Nile crocodiles in Africa — they can measure up to 6 metres in length.

Nile crocodiles are expert hunters. Many of them have had a long time to practise, as they can live for up to 100 years!

RUNNING WITH THE
WILDEBEEST, KENYA

Every year, the Mara River in East Africa becomes the scene of one of nature's most spectacular events. Between July and September, thousands of wildebeest, zebras and gazelles are on the move, leaving behind them the dry, scorched grasses of the Serengeti and following the rains north to the lush landscapes of the Masai Mara. But on their long journey they face a big problem: the Mara River blocks their way.

The late-summer rains swell the river until it becomes a foaming torrent; a deadly barrier between the herds and the rich grazing beyond. But every creature must take the plunge. On the way, the frail, weak or young may be picked off by the enormous Nile crocodiles that lurk in the swirling waters, or the hungry lions that stalk the banks beyond. In this fight for life, only the strong – or the very lucky – will survive.

HANGING OUT WITH THE
FRUIT BATS, ZAMBIA

Each November and December, a very special event takes place in a small area of forest in Zambia's Kasanka National Park. About 8 million straw-coloured fruit bats gather in a clump of trees the size of a few football pitches! This is, in fact, the largest mammal migration anywhere on Earth. So why do they come? At this time of year, the forest has a bumper crop of tasty fruits, so the bats flock to devour waterberries, mangos, masukus and milkwood berries. During the day, the bats crowd each other, elbowing and shoving to find a spare inch of branch from which to hang. They doze for hours, their wings tucked neatly beside their honey-coloured bellies. But as twilight falls, they head out for the feast. The skies become thick with clouds of wings as these furry fruit-guzzlers take off in their millions!

A bat can gobble up to twice its body weight in fruit each night.

The fruit bat's nose is crammed full of sensors, allowing it to sniff out food from several kilometres away.

In terms of numbers, this bat migration is even bigger than the world-famous wildebeest migration between Tanzania and Kenya.

The straw-coloured fruit bat is one of the largest bats in Africa — its wingspan can reach up to 85 centimetres!

Claws on the wings are the bat's extended thumbs!

Large, sensitive ears help the bat detect predators

Curved claws allow bat to hang from a branch

Leathery wings stretched across 'finger' bones

In the shadows of the trees, crocodiles and pythons lurk, eager to snap up any bats that end up on the ground.

A branch may become so weighed down by sleeping bats that it snaps!

Where do the bats come from? They possibly fly in from a neighbouring country: the Democratic Republic of the Congo.

The fruit bat has claws on its wings, which allow it to clamber among tree branches.

The African rock python is Africa's largest snake. It can grow up to 7 metres long — nearly as long as a bus!

Kasanka National Park

ZAMBIA

13

BATTLING WITH THE
HIPPOS, BOTSWANA

The Kalahari Desert in Southern Africa receives no rainfall for months at a time, yet it is home to one of the world's most iconic water-dwelling animals: the hippo. Unlike most rivers, which lead to the sea, the Okavango River empties onto open land in an area of Botswana known as the Okavango Delta. Once a year, after the summer rains, this life-saving flood turns 10,000 square kilometres of scorched plains into a watery animal haven. Here, a group of female hippos gather in a pod led by a dominant male. He is prepared to fight off all competition to keep his mates for himself. If another male approaches, the rivals square up, opening wide their mouths to bare their tusks. Then they wrestle, pushing each other to and fro with powerful jaws. Such fights can go on for hours, but there can only be one winner. The loser may be left seriously injured, while the victor will face many more battles if he is going to hold on to his territory...

At sunset, the hippos leave the group and wander off on their own to graze on grasses.

With eyes, ears and nostrils positioned high on its head, the hippo can stay alert to danger and breathe while the rest of its body is underwater.

Up to 30 hippos live together in a group, or pod, led by a dominant male. Sticking together helps keep the hippos safe from crocodiles.

Eyes, ears and nostrils on top of head

Hairless skin produces oily liquid that acts like sun cream

Mouth can open 1.2 metres wide!

Webbed toes help hippo paddle through water

A hippo can move quickly on land if it needs to escape from danger, reaching speeds of over 30 kilometres per hour.

Okavango Delta

BOTSWANA

Birds called oxpeckers sometimes help keep an injured hippo's wounds clean by pecking away any rotten flesh.

Hippos spend most of the day submerged in the water. This keeps them cool and allows them to save their energy for night-time feeding.

One of the most dangerous African animals, the hippo will warn off a rival by displaying its large canine teeth. If this fails, it uses these tusks to stab its opponent.

A young hippo will sometimes climb onto its mother's back for safety.

A hippo's ears and nostrils close up underwater. It can stay submerged for five minutes.

Hippos can sleep underwater, bobbing up to the surface for air without waking up!

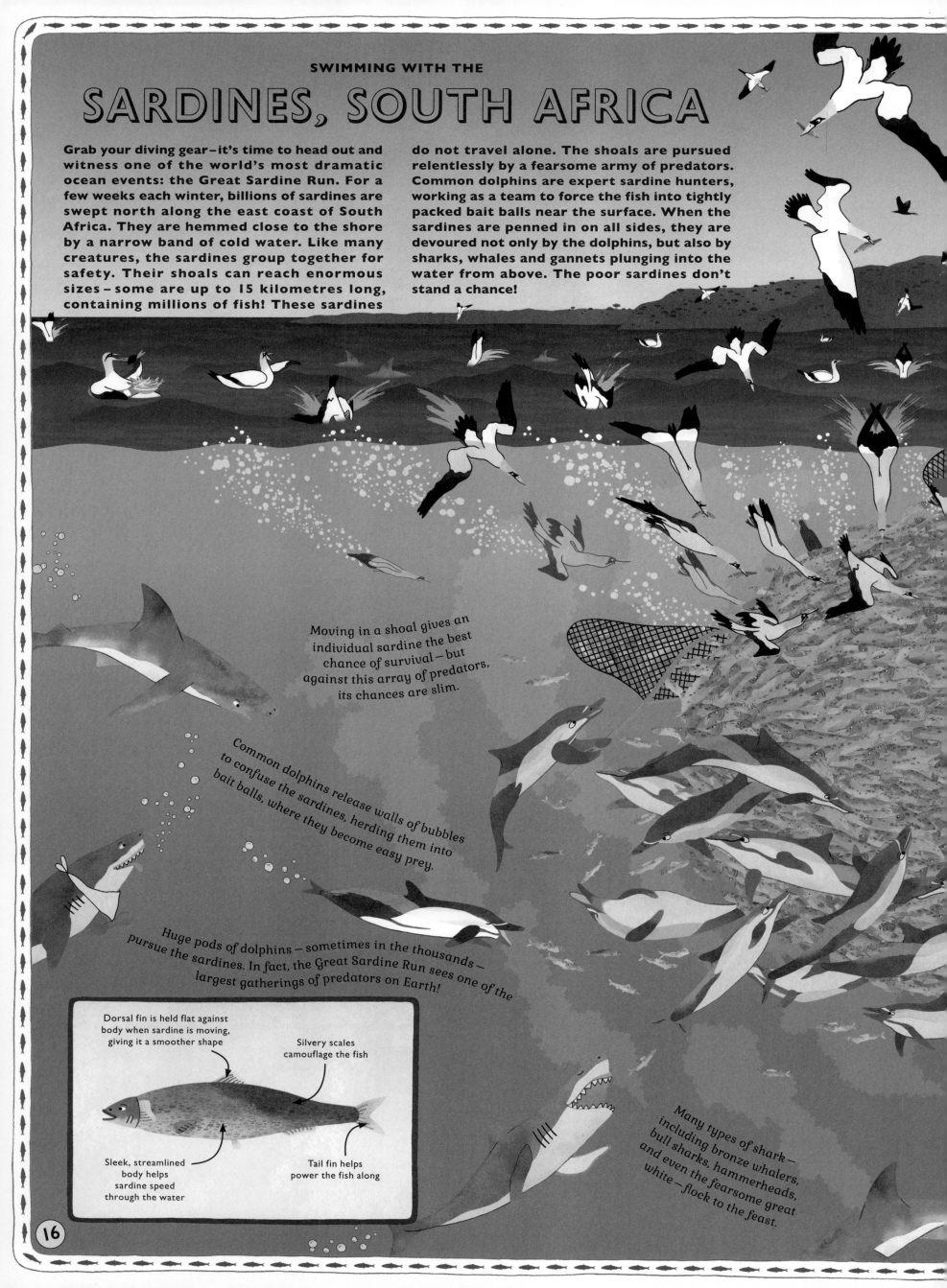

SARDINES, SOUTH AFRICA

Grab your diving gear–it's time to head out and witness one of the world's most dramatic ocean events: the Great Sardine Run. For a few weeks each winter, billions of sardines are swept north along the east coast of South Africa. They are hemmed close to the shore by a narrow band of cold water. Like many creatures, the sardines group together for safety. Their shoals can reach enormous sizes – some are up to 15 kilometres long, containing millions of fish! These sardines do not travel alone. The shoals are pursued relentlessly by a fearsome army of predators. Common dolphins are expert sardine hunters, working as a team to force the fish into tightly packed bait balls near the surface. When the sardines are penned in on all sides, they are devoured not only by the dolphins, but also by sharks, whales and gannets plunging into the water from above. The poor sardines don't stand a chance!

Moving in a shoal gives an individual sardine the best chance of survival – but against this array of predators, its chances are slim.

Common dolphins release walls of bubbles to confuse the sardines, herding them into bait balls, where they become easy prey.

Huge pods of dolphins – sometimes in the thousands – pursue the sardines. In fact, the Great Sardine Run sees one of the largest gatherings of predators on Earth!

Dorsal fin is held flat against body when sardine is moving, giving it a smoother shape

Silvery scales camouflage the fish

Sleek, streamlined body helps sardine speed through the water

Tail fin helps power the fish along

Many types of shark – including bronze whalers, bull sharks, hammerheads, and even the fearsome great white – flock to the feast.

Perhaps because of the world's changing climate, the
Sardine Run is not totally predictable. Some years,
it doesn't appear to happen at all.

The breeding season of these gannets is timed
to tie in with the arrival of the sardines so the birds
have plenty of fresh fish to feed their young.

SOUTH AFRICA

Sardine
Run

Greedy gannets wait until the dolphins have
driven the sardines up to the surface. Then they swoop
in from above, dive-bombing the shoal.

Gannets can plummet from
30 metres above the surface at
a speed of 160 kilometres per
hour, diving up to 12 metres
underwater!

Dolphins use a special technique called echolocation to
hunt: they send out clicks and listen for the echoes to
bounce back. These tell them where to find their prey.

The largest predator in this deadly army is the solitary
Bryde's whale. This sleek sardine-lover can measure
15 metres in length – nearly as long as two tennis courts!

17

HATCHING WITH THE
GREEN SEA TURTLES, WEST AFRICA

The moment a baby green sea turtle is born, it begins the most important journey of its life: a sprint from its nest in the sand to the safety of the ocean. Unlike some creatures, whose mothers help them hatch, green sea turtles must make their way out of their shells on their own. Using a sharp tooth called a caruncle, which disappears soon after the turtles hatch, the youngsters dig themselves free from the nest over many days. They emerge from the sands along with hundreds of others. Then they turn to face the brightest horizon – the sea – and they're off! On this journey, the hatchlings dodge and dash past predators such as yellow-billed kites, crows and ghost crabs, all of whom are looking for a meal. In this race, every turtle that makes it to the ocean is a winner!

Female sea turtles lay their eggs on land. A female can lay up to 200 eggs in one nest!

Hatchlings can sleep floating on the water's surface with their front flippers folded over their backs.

Adult green turtles are vegetarian, eating sea grasses and algae, but the youngsters feed on small fish, crabs and jellyfish.

With their paddle-like flippers, adult green sea turtles can swim at speeds of up to 56 kilometres per hour.

A green sea turtle is able to hold its breath for hours at a time.

Sharks, large fish and circling birds all prey on baby turtles, so the hatchlings must take care underwater as well as on land.

When born, these turtles are only 5 centimetres long, but they can grow up to 1.5 metres in length and over 300 kilograms in weight — as heavy as a full-grown zebra!

AFRICA

Turtle beaches

To nest, most female sea turtles return to the very beach where they hatched!

Sea turtles travel long distances, often hundreds of kilometres, between their feeding and nesting grounds.

The green turtle isn't named after the colour of its shell, which is usually brown, but after the colour of the green fat beneath its shell.

Under threat because of the destruction of its nesting areas, the green sea turtle is an endangered species.

Tough outer shell, called a carapace, for protection

Unlike a tortoise, the green sea turtle can't pull its head or legs inside its shell

Rear flippers act as rudders, for steering

Front flippers propel turtle along

Exploring with the
POLAR BEARS (Greenland)

Nesting with the
PUFFINS (Iceland)

Iceland

Faroe Islands

Shetland Islands

EUROPE

Over a quarter of Europe is covered in woodland. Its ancient forests, dramatic mountain landscapes and lush grasslands are havens for wildlife and – in the far north – rare creatures such as wolves and polar bears still roam.

Migrating
with the
EELS (Norway)

Norway

Rutting with
the STAGS
(Britain)

United
Kingdom

Denmark

Ireland

Moving house with the
HONEYBEES (British Isles)

Netherlands

Luxembourg

Belgium

North
Atlantic
Ocean

France

Rock-hopping
with the
ALPINE IBEX
(Germany)

Liechtenstein

Switzerland

Changing shape
with the
MARBLED NEWT
(Portugal)

Night flying
with the
BARN OWLS
(France)

Italy

Monaco

San
Marino

Spain

Portugal

Parading
with the
PROCESSIONARY
CATERPILLARS
(Spain)

Mediterranean
Sea

Corsica

Vatican
City

Balearic
Islands

Sardinia

Africa

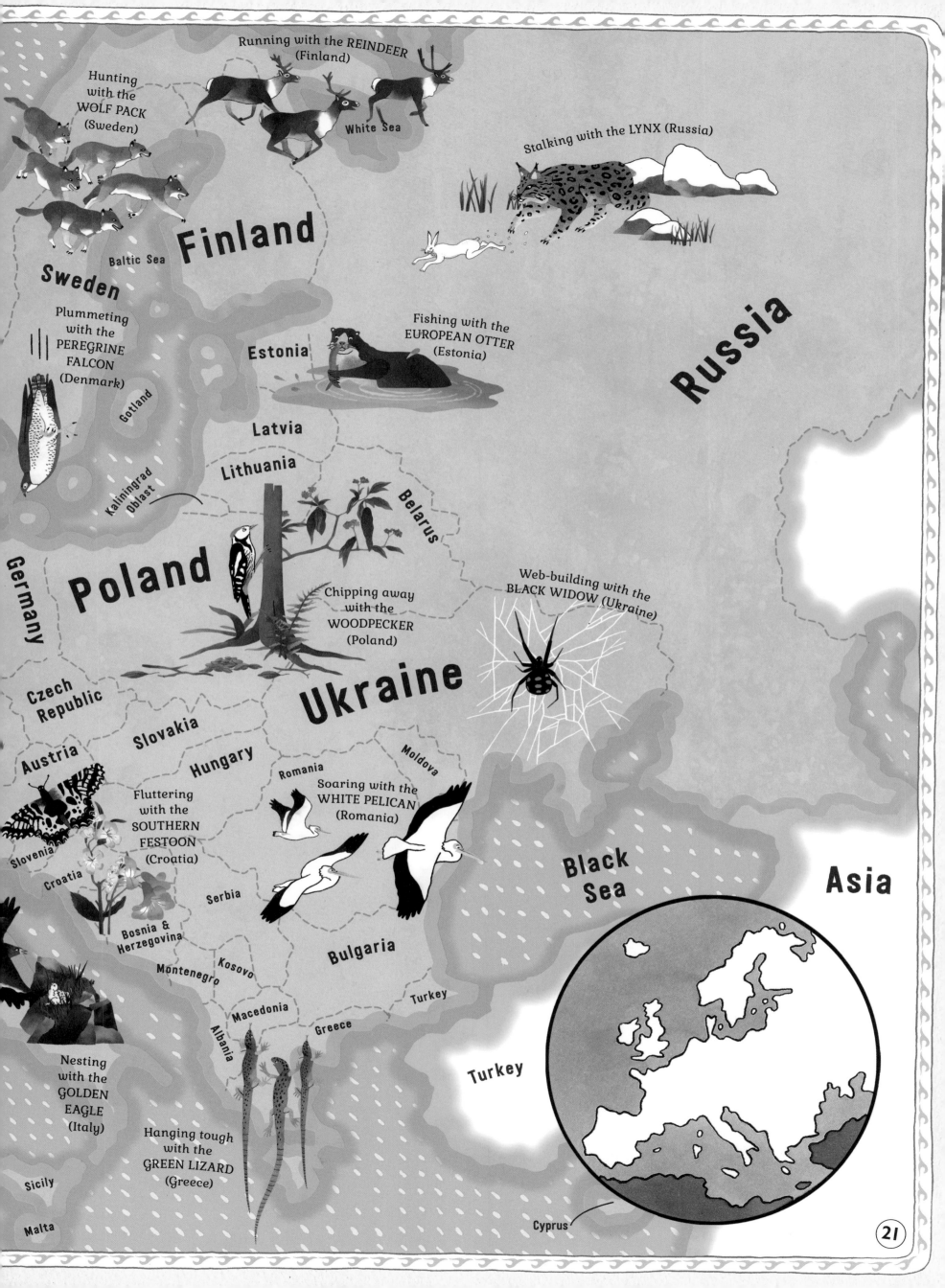

Running with the REINDEER
(Finland)

Hunting with the WOLF PACK
(Sweden)

White Sea

Stalking with the LYNX (Russia)

Finland

Baltic Sea

Sweden

Fishing with the
EUROPEAN OTTER
(Estonia)

Russia

Plummeting
with the
PEREGRINE
FALCON
(Denmark)

Estonia

Gotland

Latvia

Lithuania

Kaliningrad
Oblast

Belarus

Germany

Poland

Web-building with the
BLACK WIDOW (Ukraine)

Chipping away
with the
WOODPECKER
(Poland)

Czech
Republic

Ukraine

Slovakia

Austria

Hungary

Moldova

Romania

Soaring with the
WHITE PELICAN
(Romania)

Slovenia

Fluttering
with the
SOUTHERN
FESTOON
(Croatia)

Croatia

Serbia

Bosnia &
Herzegovina

Kosovo

**Black
Sea**

Asia

Montenegro

Bulgaria

Nesting
with the
GOLDEN
EAGLE
(Italy)

Macedonia

Turkey

Albania

Greece

Turkey

Hanging tough
with the
GREEN LIZARD
(Greece)

Sicily

Cyprus

Malta

21

Polar bear habitat

GREENLAND

When they are born, the cubs are helpless and blind. They open their eyes after a month, and emerge from the den at about three months old.

Polar bears don't have many predators, but cubs are sometimes hunted by Arctic wolves.

Seal breathing holes are prime hunting spots for polar bears.

As the world's climate warms, the ice caps melt, which puts polar bears at risk because they need ice shelves in order to hunt.

A large male polar bear can weigh 720 kilograms, which is nearly as heavy as a small car! The females weigh half as much.

Dense fur and thick layer of fat stop bear from getting cold

Large, splayed feet stop bear from sinking into snow

Powerful nose can detect a seal from over a kilometre away

Fur grows even on base of paws to keep them warm and help bear grip the ice

POLAR BEARS, GREENLAND

Emerging from a warm, dark den into the bright, freezing air of an Arctic spring must be a bit of a shock for a baby polar bear! In the winter, a female polar bear digs herself a den under the deep snow. Here, she gives birth to her cubs. The mother's body heat keeps the cubs warm, while her rich milk helps them grow. When spring comes, the youngsters finally peek out for the first time. For the next week or so, the mother takes the cubs on short trips away from the den so they can get used to their new surroundings. But it's not all fun and games: the mother is hungry – she hasn't eaten for months and has lost half her body weight. Once the little ones are ready, the family must make the long walk to the sea ice, where they can hunt for seals. But the journey will be dangerous: the cubs may be preyed on by wolves or even by other polar bears. The mother will need to keep her wits about her to protect her little ones.

A polar bear can carry her cubs on her back through deep snow or water.

Brrrrr! Even in spring, temperatures can be as low as -20° Celsius! The cubs must stay close to their mother to keep warm.

The cubs learn to catch seals by watching their mother. They will stay with her until they are two or three years old.

To catch a seal, a bear lurks by the edge of the ice, waiting for its prey to surface. Then it pounces, snatching the seal onto the ice with its huge claws.

Polar bears are fantastic swimmers. Their front paws are slightly webbed, which helps them paddle through the water.

The spring sun shines on the sea ice, melting it. The polar bears must make it to the sea before the ice breaks up, or they won't be able to hunt seals.

Látrabjarg
Bird Cliffs

ICELAND

Birds of a feather flock together... The different species of bird here all nest at different heights on the jagged cliffs.

Because guillemots nest on sheer cliff ledges, their eggs have a conelike shape. This means they won't roll away over the edge!

In the past, local people would abseil down the cliff faces to gather eggs to eat.

These cliffs are home to the largest colony of razorbills in the world.

Did you know... a baby puffin is called a puffling!

A puffin's beak can carry a mouthful of fish — a single bird has been known to hold 62 fish at once!

24

PUFFINS, ICELAND

The westernmost tip of Iceland hosts a wildlife spectacle not to be missed. Every summer, the Látrabjarg Bird Cliffs become home to millions of nesting birds, squawking, squabbling and shrieking. On the soaring 440-metre-high cliff faces you will find the nests of guillemots, razorbills and kittiwakes. But the stars of the show are the colourful puffins who make their burrows on the grassy cliff tops. They dig into the soil using their beaks as picks and their feet as spades, flinging the earth out behind them. Once a burrow is ready, a female will lay a single egg at the back, on a bed of feathers.

The male and female share the jobs of keeping the egg warm and finding food for the young chick once it hatches. Puffins are not the most graceful of fliers: it often takes a bit of effort to get off the ground, but – once airborne – they can soar at surprising speeds of up to 88 kilometres per hour! More than half of the world's entire population of Atlantic puffins breeds in Iceland, so grab your binoculars and get puffin-spotting!

Watch out! One of the main predators of the puffin is the great black-backed gull, which may swoop down to seize young chicks.

Puffins usually keep the same mate and return to the same burrow every year.

Puffins can stay underwater for up to a minute, diving to catch fish to eat.

At the foot of the cliffs, the smell of guano – otherwise known as bird poo – can be quite overwhelming!

Colourful beak turns brighter in breeding season

Wings are used in flight and to propel puffin through the water

Roof of beak is lined with spines that hold fish in place while puffin catches more

Strong legs are used as a rudder while swimming

BRITISH ISLES

Honeybee habitat

A larva's future job is determined at just four days old, and depends on what it is fed. A diet of bee bread (mainly pollen) will mean it becomes a worker or a drone.

The honeybee lives in a group called a colony, which can contain up to 80,000 bees during the summer.

Most bees are female workers. Their jobs involve collecting pollen and nectar, storing honey, nursing the young, building and cleaning the hive, guarding the nest and feeding the queen!

The queen lays up to 2,000 eggs a day during the summer. That's more than her whole body weight in eggs each day!

HONEYBEES, THE BRITISH ISLES

Workers create a new queen by producing a special food called royal jelly and feeding it to some of the larvae.

As summer creeps across the countryside of the British Isles, the honeybees are keeping busy. The female workers are foraging, guarding the colony and feeding the young grubs, called larvae. The queen bee is the only egg-layer in the hive. She communicates with the workers using signals called pheromones. But as the larvae grow up and the hive gets bigger, not all the bees have access to the queen, so they don't all get her messages. For them, this means the queen no longer exists, so they set about creating a new one! As there can only be one queen in a colony, the existing queen leaves. She flies off, followed by a swarm. The swarm clings to a branch not far from the original hive and clusters around the queen to protect her. Meanwhile, scout bees set out to find the perfect spot to set up a new hive.

If two queens hatch at the same time, they may fight to the death!

Scout bees perform a set of movements called a waggle dance to direct the other bees to their new home.

The queen bee is the largest bee in the colony – about twice the length of the workers.

Male bees are called drones, and their only job is to mate with the queen so she can lay eggs. In autumn, the workers push them out of the hive and they freeze to death.

A bee sucks up a flower's nectar using its long tongue. The bee takes it back to the hive, where it is made into honey, which will feed the bees during winter.

Workers carry pollen using baskets on their legs. Some pollen rubs off as they visit flowers, helping fertilise them. If bees died out, many plants would too.

Types of Honeybee

| Worker | Drone | Queen |

NIGHT FLYING WITH

BARN OWLS, FRANCE

As dusk settles on the lavender field of Provence, one creature is dusting off it's biggest asset: its feathers. Barns owls have plumage that absorbs high-frequency sound that most prey as well as humans cannot hear.

Their large wings also support a lightweight body, allowing them to fly very slowly and hover over a potential meal. Nesting during the summer months when their food of mice and other rodents are plentiful, males are the primary hunters for this season as their little owlets enter the world.

Nightjars can also be spotted in this area, using their sophisticated flying abilities to hunt at dawn and dusk.

Barn owls are also known to feed on rats, small rabbits and bats.

These owls' lopsided ears help them to pinpoint exactly where tiny sounds are coming from.

On a good night, a barn owl will catch 3 to 4 prey.

Heart-shaped face collects sound

Flexible neck allows the owl to turn its head 180 degrees

Light body, big wings and soft feathers help the owl to fly silently

Sharp talons and powerful feet for catching prey

The world-famous lavender farms of the region have been an essential part of French cuisine and scented goods for hundreds of years.

Baby barn owls will be ready to hunt when they are 8 weeks old.

These owls make nests in trees, chimneys, ... and in barns!

Sometimes, owlets feed each other in their nests — a rare trait amongst predatory birds.

FRANCE

Provence

29

Freshwater-living with the
BAIKAL SEALS (Russia)

Russia

Flocking with the
FLAMINGOS (Turkey)

Huddling together
with the YAKS
(Mongolia)

Europe

Kazakhstan

Mongolia

Black Sea

Azerbaijan

Georgia

Armenia

Caspian Sea

Turkey

Uzbekistan

Kyrgyzstan

China

Turkmenistan

Tajikistan

Palestine

Syria

Lebanon

Israel

Jordan

Iraq

Iran

Swarming with the
DESERT LOCUSTS
(Saudi Arabia)

Afghanistan

Crevasse-leaping
with the
SNOW
LEOPARDS
(Nepal)

Preening parties
with the
GOLDEN
SNUB-NOSED
MONKEYS
(China)

Kuwait

Bahrain

Qatar

United Arab
Emirates

Pakistan

India

Nepal

Bhutan

India

Bangladesh

Myanmar

**Saudi
Arabia**

Striking out
with the
KING COBRA
(India)

Termite-hunting
with the PANGOLINS
(Cambodia)

Filter-feeding with the
WHALE SHARKS
(Oman)

Reef-roving
with the
ANGELFISH
(Thailand)

Oman

Yemen

Arabian Sea

Parading with the
PEACOCKS
(India)

**Bay of
Bengal**

Thailand

Africa

Gathering with
the ELEPHANTS
(Sri Lanka)

Malaysia

Indonesia

**Indian
Ocean**

Sri Lanka

Flights of fancy
with the
MOON MOTH
(Malaysia)

Maldives

Seychelles

Chagos Archipelago

ASIA & THE MIDDLE EAST

The size of the world's largest continent explains its astonishing array of wildlife. Reaching almost halfway round the globe, Asia is home to a whole host of creatures, from the mighty Siberian tiger to the mischievous orang-utan and the elusive giant panda.

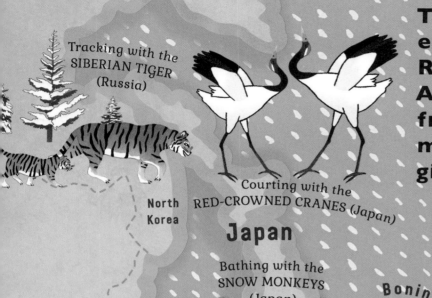

Tracking with the SIBERIAN TIGER (Russia)

Courting with the RED-CROWNED CRANES (Japan)

North Korea

Japan

Bathing with the SNOW MONKEYS (Japan)

Bonin Islands

South Korea

North Pacific Ocean

Mountain-climbing with the GIANT PANDAS (China)

Volcano Islands

Taiwan

East China Sea

Tree-dwelling with the MOON BEARS (Laos)

Clever camouflage with the LEAF INSECTS (Philippines)

South China Sea

Philippines

Laos

Vietnam

Cambodia

Brunei

Sabah

Singapore

Sarawak

Indonesian Borneo

Sulawesi

Papua

Bringing up baby with the ORANG-UTANS (Borneo)

Celebes

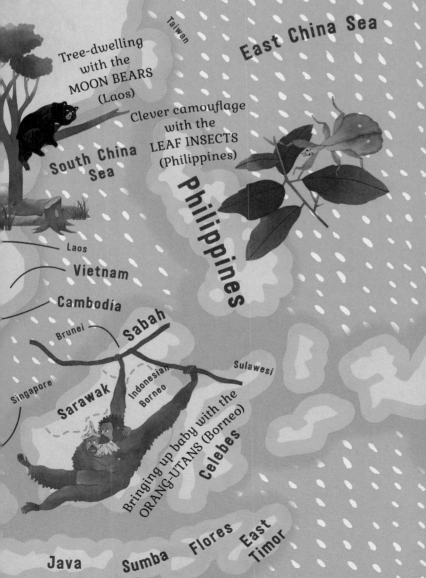

Java   Sumba   Flores   East Timor

RUSSIA

Siberian tiger habitat

A female tiger will carry her young cubs in her mouth if she feels they are in danger.

The tiger tends to hunt at night, using its excellent sight and hearing. It can see six times better than a human in the dark.

While raising her young, a tiger must kill an animal every five days to give them all enough energy to survive.

Tiger cubs leave their mother at about three years of age. They must now establish their own territory, leaving scents by scratching and rubbing against trees.

TRACKING WITH THE

SIBERIAN TIGER, RUSSIA

Winters in far-eastern Russia are long and harsh. Snow and ice grip the land and temperatures plummet to -40° Celsius. A female tiger must provide plenty of food to keep her young cubs going through the freezing months. When the tiger cubs are between three and six months old, their constant demands for milk begin to irritate their mother, so she must teach them to hunt. With her cubs tumbling playfully at her heels, the mother leads them through the dark, snowy forest, following the scent of a young deer. When the tiger stops suddenly, so do the cubs, their heads cocked to one side, listening. They follow their mother, keeping low, out of sight. The tiger must get within 18 metres of her victim before pouncing, otherwise the deer might outrun her. Finally, when she is close enough, she hurtles forward, seizing the deer with a quick bite to the throat. The cubs look on, an important lesson learned.

Stripes break up the outline of the tiger's body so it can avoid being seen by prey

No two tigers have the same pattern of stripes

Strong legs for running and jumping: at full speed, the tiger can run at speeds up to 64 kilometres per hour!

Sensitive whiskers help a tiger find its way through the dark forest.

A tiger cub will not make a large kill of its own until it is about 18 months old. It must practise on smaller targets beforehand.

The tiger is equipped with huge canine teeth and long claws to grab and hold prey.

Siberian tigers are the biggest cats in the world. The male can weigh over 300 kilograms – that's the same as about ten 10-year-olds!

Despite their famous strength, Siberian tigers are endangered. There are fewer than 500 left in the wild.

Male courtship dance

The ritual begins with his back to the female

Turning around, he fans his feathers wide

Shown here in the Taj Umaid Rajasthan, Bhawan Palace in Rajasthan, peacocks roam the floral palace freely.

Peahens choose their mates according to size and quality of the male's feathers.

The shimmer in a peacock's feathers comes from crystal-like structures that reflect light waves, attractive to peahens — and humans!

PARADING WITH

PEACOCKS, INDIA

Few species of bird take courtship as seriously as the Indian peafowl. Known more commonly as the peacock, the male of this species is also the national bird of India, and the proud owner of an aquamarine tail feather that he uses to show his strength as a male and attract potential mates. His tail feather is covered in colourful 'eye' markings of blue, gold and red hues, and when spread out, it covers more than 60 percent of the bird's total body length. With his back to the female, the male raises his iridescent tail into a full fan and shakes his undergarments in the direction of onlookers. With a confident twist, he turns to face a potential mate, shaking his magnificent plumage as he works his way towards her. Scientists has proven that females choose their mates according to the size, colour and quality of the male's tail feather.

In India, peacocks are considered to be sacred.

Female peafowls are called peahens.

Peacocks are among one of the world's largest flying birds.

Peacocks eat seeds, plants, insects and small reptiles.

Male peachicks don't start growing their showy trains until about age three.

The peacock's plumage looks its best when the male reaches the age of 5 or 6.

Peahens are mostly dull brown or grey with short feathers.

Rajasthan

INDIA

INDIA

Minneriya
National
Park

SRI
LANKA

Over 130 species of bird inhabit this national park, including herons, pelicans and peacocks.

The Sri Lankan leopard hunts at night and dozes in a tree during the day.

The sloth bear is a noisy feeder, grunting and slurping as it guzzles fruit and termites.

The blue peacock can be found here in all its glory, showing off its distinctive tail fan of blue, gold and green.

Elephants are fond of a shower. They use their trunks to suck up water, then squirt it all over themselves — and each other!

Despite its size, the Asian elephant is a quiet mover thanks to its wide, padded feet.

Elephants have longer pregnancies than any other land animal — about 22 months — so having a baby is a big commitment!

Each summer, around 300 elephants travel from across the region to enjoy the waters of the Minneriya reservoir.

Trunk can measure up to 2 metres and hold 4 litres of water; great for squirting!

Very intelligent animal with large brain

Tusks used as a foraging tool and for defence

Spotted deer feed close to the water. They must take care because they are a favourite meal of the leopard!

Asian elephants are not quite as large as their African cousins, and can be identified by their smaller, rounded ears.

The trunk of an elephant is an amazing tool: it is used for drinking, washing, smelling, breathing and grabbing things — including a meal!

GATHERING WITH THE

ELEPHANTS, SRI LANKA

Every year, there is one important social event that the elephants of northern Sri Lanka do not want to miss: the gathering at the ancient reservoir in the Minneriya National Park. Each summer for hundreds of years, herds of elephants have made the trek here to bathe, feed, socialize and find a mate. During the dry season, the park's green grasses provide the elephants with plenty of food, while the reservoir's waters are deep enough for even the largest members of the herd to take a cooling bath. Also invited to the party, spotted deer, sloth bears, leopards and more than a dozen species of bird look on as the world's greatest gathering of Asian elephants takes place.

In the wild, giant pandas live only in a few remote mountain ranges of central China.

CHINA

Giant panda habitat

This solitary creature is considered one of the shyest and rarest animals in the world.

Giant pandas are endangered: there are only about 1,500 left in the wild.

The giant panda usually lives alone, but it communicates with others using calls and scents.

Giant pandas are skilled tree climbers and strong swimmers.

MOUNTAIN-CLIMBING WITH THE
GIANT PANDAS, CHINA

It is nearly summer in the foothills of the Qinling Mountains in China, and the giant panda is on its way to higher ground in search of one thing: juicy bamboo leaves. For a creature who must eat a lot to maintain its huge body weight, the panda's trek up the mountains is essential. Throughout spring, the bear has been munching wood bamboo shoots in the lower valleys, but as June arrives, these mature, providing fewer nutrients. The panda must climb the slopes to seek out arrow bamboo leaves, which are rich in calcium. Unlike other bears, which eat a variety of foods, giant pandas feed almost only on bamboo. It is astonishing that these large creatures can survive on such a meagre diet, but they do – and the key to this survival is laziness! Instead of chasing their dinner, pandas spend a lot of time moving very slowly, meaning that they use up much less energy than other creatures their size. In fact, they spend up to 17 hours a day just sitting and munching bamboo!

The Qinling Mountains are home to between 200 and 300 giant pandas.

Habitat loss and poaching have become major threats to the panda. New reserves and forest corridors have been created in an effort to preserve these extraordinary creatures.

Female pandas raise their cubs on their own, and babies stay with their mother for the first 18 months of their life.

Giant pandas have a piece of wrist bone on each paw that sticks out like a thumb, helping them grab and tear bamboo.

Pandas have to eat about 20 kilograms of bamboo per day to survive!

The bears drink fresh water from rivers and streams. In addition to bamboo, they may sometimes eat small rodents or other grasses. They even lick rocks for extra nutrients!

The Life Cycle of a Giant Panda

Newborn: 0–4 months

Cubhood: 4–24 months

Independence: 1.5 / 2 years

Maturity: 4 / 6 years

Humans share 96% of their genetic make-up with orang-utans!

A baby orang-utan will cling to its mother's stomach, sides or back while she swings through the trees.

Some baby orang-utans breastfeed from their mothers for 8 years!

The jungles of Borneo are also home to macaques and other monkeys.

Like humans, the orang-utan uses tools to get food from hard-to-reach places. It forces open the husk of the Neesia fruit with a stick.

The clouded leopard is the orang-utan's greatest enemy in the Borneo jungle.

Orang-utan habitat

BORNEO

ORANG-UTANS, BORNEO

There is one creature where the bond between mother and child is thought to be just as strong as in humans: the orang-utan. The island of Borneo is one of the only places in the world where these affectionate apes live in the wild. Here you will find mothers so attached to their babies that they carry them constantly for the first four months. Until they are two, the youngsters are totally dependent on their mother both for food and transport. In fact, many will be carried until they are five! This kind of intense bond is very rare among animals. It's thought that orang-utans have such long childhoods because there is so much to learn before they can live alone. Mothers teach their babies what to eat, where to find it, and who to avoid. Even when they finally become independent at around the age of 10, orang-utans will often come back to see their mums – usually just in time for a good meal!

These nimble climbers rest in a sleeping nest carefully woven from sticks and leaves.

'Orang-utan' means 'person of the forest' in the Malay language.

Orang-utans eat bark, leaves, flowers, insects and – most importantly – lots of fruit!

Orang-utans are members of the great ape family, along with gorillas, chimpanzees, bonobos... and humans!

The great apes are the only creatures who have been found to respond to being tickled!

Arms are longer than legs; perfect for swinging through the trees

Orange-reddish hair colour

Can grasp with hands or feet

AUSTRALASIA & OCEANIA

The world's smallest continent packs a powerful punch where wildlife is concerned. With its tropical oceans, colourful rainforests and spectacular mountains, Australasia has some of the most unusual and fascinating wildlife on Earth.

Showing off
with the
BIRDS OF PARADISE
(Papua New Guinea)

Daddy day care
with the
CASSOWARIES
(Australia)

Indonesia

Papua New Guinea

Reef-living
with the
MANDARIN FISH
(Australia)

Christmas Island

Braving traffic
with the
RED CRABS
(Christmas Island)

Australia

Building with the
BOWERBIRDS
(Australia)

Diving with the
PLATYPUS
(Australia)

Coming home with the
FAIRY PENGUINS (Australia)

Boxing with the
KANGAROOS (Australia)

Burrowing with the
WOMBATS (Australia)

Flinders Island

Hissing and howling
with the
TASMANIAN DEVILS
(Tasmania)

Tasmania

Calving with the
SOUTHERN RIGHT WHALES
(New Zealand)

Hawaiian Islands

Following fishing boats
with the BOTTLENOSE DOLPHINS
(Hawaiian Islands)

Federated States
of Micronesia

Marshall
Islands

Puffing up with the
PUFFERFISH (Tuvalu)

Passing through
with the
LEATHERBACK TURTLES
(French Polynesia)

Snacking on
sharks with the
SALTWATER CROCODILE
(Solomon Islands)

Solomon
Islands

Tuvalu

Vanuatu

New
Caledonia

Pillaging pollen
with the
RAINBOW LORIKEETS
(Vanuatu)

Cracking shells
with the
GIANT COCONUT CRAB
(Samoa)

French
Polynesia

Evading hunters
with the
FLYING FISH (Fiji)

Samoa

Fiji

Tonga

Norfolk Island

Grub-grabbing
with the KIWIS
(New Zealand)

Kermadec Islands

New
Zealand

HITTING THE DANCE FLOOR WITH THE
BIRDS OF PARADISE, NEW GUINEA

High in the hilltop rainforests of New Guinea, you will find a dance floor devoted to an extraordinary creature: the bird of paradise. With feathers that extend from his beak, wings and head, the male of this family makes his own stage on a tree trunk or a patch of dry ground. He shows off his colourful plumage with special moves to attract females.

After meticulously preparing his dance floor, the male calls out to the ladies of the rainforest, letting them know the show is about to begin. Each species performs a unique dance: the superb bird of paradise fans out his plumage and snaps his tail feathers against each other as he hops about in circles; the western parotia does a ballet-like dance, shaking his neck to show off his brilliant head feathers; while the blue bird of paradise hangs upside down to create an arch with his long tail feathers. What a show!

The female superb bird of paradise builds a nest and cares for the young on her own.

New Guinea is the world's largest and highest tropical island, and one of the most biodiverse places on Earth.

The average female superb bird of paradise rejects up to 20 suitors before finding a mate.

There are over 700 species of butterfly in New Guinea.

Superb Bird of Paradise Dance

First, the male prepares his dance floor.

His blue breast shield springs up...

followed by his black cape.

Then he hops in circles around the female.

Bird of paradise habitat

The western parotia has several long plumes that grow from behind each eye.

The male blue bird of paradise hums to the female as he hangs upside down.

Some displays by the male birds can last for hours!

To prepare his dance floor, a male may go so far as scrubbing the area with leaves.

When the superb bird of paradise's feathers are outstretched, he begins his hopping dance.

The superb bird of paradise species has an unusually low number of females, so competition among males for mates is fierce!

These tropical forests are so rich in fruit that a few minutes of feeding can fuel the birds for a whole day – leaving plenty of time for bower building!

The Vogelkop bowerbird's bower takes years to build. His thatched tent sits on a mossy lawn decorated with flowers.

BUILDING WITH THE

BOWERBIRDS, NEW GUINEA & AUSTRALIA

In the forests of New Guinea and Australia, one of the most unusual courtship rituals in the world takes place. Here, you may come across a master of building and home decoration: the bowerbird. This cousin of the bird of paradise shows off some unexpected skills to attract a mate. First, he builds a bower out of twigs. This isn't a nest – this is his showcase to impress the ladies! Once the bower is complete, the male decorates it with colourful objects. He spends hours scouring the forest for trinkets: berries, feathers, stones, flowers and even bottle tops, drinking straws and other plastic knick-knacks. To find a mate, a female tours the nearby bowers, checking to see which meets her high standards. Each time a female appears, the male puffs up his feathers, flicks his wings and makes buzzing noises, all in order to thrill her. The male with the most impressive bower and display is the one who will bag the most mates. May the best bird win!

NEW GUINEA

Bowerbird habitat

AUSTRALIA

Some males, such as the flame bowerbird, dance to attract females into their bowers. They even hold berries in their beaks while flapping their wings in display!

Most female bowerbirds rear their chicks on their own, but green catbirds like to do things differently...

The male doesn't build a bower structure—he just dances to attract a mate—and the pair stay together to bring up the babies!

A female bowerbird is often dull in colour compared with the male.

It is sometimes the duller-coloured males that build the most impressive bowers!

If a male bowerbird manages to impress a female, she will step into his bower and they will mate.

Some males destroy the bowers of rivals, or even steal objects to use in their own bowers!

Male satin bowerbirds have violet-blue eyes and a blue sheen to their feathers. And what colour do they choose to decorate with? You guessed it...blue!

Many bowerbirds can mimic other sounds. Spotted bowerbirds can copy at least 16 different bird calls, as well as flapping pigeon wings and even the human voice.

Types of Bower

Maypole bower: built by placing sticks around a sapling to form a teepee

Avenue bower: has a high wall on either side and an open path down the middle

AUSTRALIA

Platypus
habitat

The azure kingfisher
often follows platypuses in
the hopes of catching fish
disturbed by them.

The platypus scoops up bits of gravel
along with its food. It uses this gravel
to help it grind up food because it
has no teeth!

When swimming, a platypus closes its eyes, ears and nostrils,
using only its sensitive bill to find its way.

A platypus can stay underwater
for up to a minute.

The male has venomous
spurs on his hind legs,
which he uses to defend
himself against predators
or other males.

Thick fur
keeps platypus
warm and dry

Tail stores fat reserves

Sensitive,
rubbery bill

Eyes and ears close
up underwater

Webbing on feet retracts
on land, helping the
platypus walk

PLATYPUS, AUSTRALIA

Which creature has the beak and flippers of a duck, the tail of a beaver and the body of an otter? The platypus! The platypus is such a bizarre-looking animal that when specimens were first sent to Europe in the late 1800s, scientists thought they were stitched-together hoaxes. The platypus is perfectly designed for its watery life on the riverbanks of Australia. To hunt, it leaves its burrow and plunges beneath the water. It is a skilful swimmer, using its webbed front feet for power, and its back feet and tail for steering. As it paddles, it moves its rubbery bill from side to side like a metal detector. This bill is covered in sensors so the platypus can feel its way around and detect prey. It scoops up mouthfuls of insects, shellfish and worms from the riverbed, coming back to the surface to chew its meal. The platypus's ducklike beak and flippers aren't the only strange things about this creature: it is also one of only two mammals on the planet to lay eggs!

The platypus is hunted by snakes, water rats, birds of prey and sometimes even crocodiles!

A newly hatched platypus is tiny—about the size of a butter bean!

To dig a burrow in a riverbank, the platypus pushes aside earth with its bill.

A female platypus lays one or two eggs in her burrow, keeping them warm against her body. The eggs hatch after about 10 days.

The mother produces milk to feed her baby. This milk doesn't come from teats, as on other mammals, but oozes straight from her skin!

Tail acts like a fifth leg, supporting the kangaroo

Joey is carried in pouch

Powerful hind legs

At full speed, a kangaroo can outrun a racehorse! It can cover 8 metres in a single leap.

There are more kangaroos than humans in Australia!

Male kangaroos are called bucks, boomers or jacks; a female is a doe, flyer or jill. And a baby is a joey!

A kick from a kangaroo's hind legs can crush bones or – in some cases – even kill an opponent.

Joeys have their own boxing matches, play fighting to practise for later in life.

Marsupials are mammals that carry their young in a pouch, and red kangaroos are the largest marsupials on Earth.

AUSTRALIA

Simpson Desert

Groups of kangaroos — called mobs — often gather at waterholes.

The kangaroo is the only large animal that uses hopping as its main way of getting around.

When it is born, a joey is a pink, hairless worm about the size of a cherry.

The tiny newborn joey climbs through its mother's fur to get to her pouch. It will stay there for several months, suckling milk.

If it is startled by something, an older joey may jump headfirst back into the pouch!

KICK-BOXING WITH THE

RED KANGAROOS, AUSTRALIA

The Australian outback is home to the country's most iconic animal: the red kangaroo. Temperatures in the Simpson Desert can reach over 50° Celsius and water is in short supply, but the bouncing roos here have some cunning ways of beating the heat. In the warmest part of the day, they take cover in the shade, digging away the topsoil to rest on the cooler earth beneath. They also have a habit of licking their wrists to cool their blood vessels. But things really start heating up when it's time to choose a mate! In a battle over a female, rival males often come to blows. A kangaroo's best weapons are its muscular hind legs and enormous feet. When fighting, two males grapple with their forearms, then deliver powerful kicks with their hind legs. The loser will retreat to lick his wounds, while the winner gets the girl!

Arctic Ocean

Greenland

Going north with the NARWHALS (Canada)

Davis Strait

Alaska (USA)

Leaping upstream with the SOCKEYE SALMON (Alaska)

Spring awakening with the AZURE BUTTERFLIES (Canada)

Gathering with the BELUGA WHALES (Canada)

Gulf of Alaska

Canada

Herding with the CARIBOU (Canada)

Hudson Bay

Tree-rubbing with the GRIZZLY BEARS (Canada)

Going the distance with the CANADA GEESE (Canada)

Fearless foraging with the WOLVERINE (United States)

Taking a dip with the mighty MOOSE (United States)

Eyeing up prey with the BALD EAGLE (United States)

Dam-building with the BEAVERS (United States)

Roaming the plains with the BISON (United States)

Sunbathing with the SWALLOWTAIL (United States)

United States of America

Climbing trees with the BLACK BEARS (United States)

Night-stalking with the OCELOT (Mexico)

Chomping leaves with the BANDED CUCUMBER BEETLE (United States)

Soulful singing with the PAINTED BUNTING (United States)

Swamp-dwelling with the ALLIGATORS (United States)

Mexico

Serious stings with the RED VELVET ANT (Mexico)

Gulf of Mexico

North Pacific Ocean

Arriving with the MONARCHS (Mexico)

NORTH AMERICA

From the icy expanses of northern Canada and Alaska to the towering mountains, wide prairies and scorching deserts of the United States, North America is bursting with breathtaking landscapes and amazing animal adventures.

North
Atlantic
Ocean

Azores

Bermuda

Sargasso
Sea

Caribbean Sea

Fish are the most important prey
for the bald eagles of Alaska.

Grizzly bears gather in the
McNeil River to wait for the
Great Salmon Run.

Often the fish leap straight
into the bears' open mouths!

Sockeye salmon are grey when young...

but turn red before they spawn

A salmon leaping up a waterfall shows
similar athletic ability to a human
hurdling a house!

ALASKA

McNeil River

Many grizzly bear families would not survive without the millions of salmon that leap upstream every year.

The name 'sockeye' is believed to come from the word 'sukkai' in British Columbia's native Coast Salish language. 'Sukkai' means red fish.

How do salmon navigate? It is thought that they use the Earth's magnetic field to find their way back to the streams where they were born.

Salmon spend their early lives in streams and rivers before they swim out to sea and grow into adults.

LEAPING UPSTREAM WITH THE

SOCKEYE SALMON, ALASKA

For the grizzly bears and bald eagles of the Alaskan wilderness, one event takes pride of place in the annual calendar: the Great Salmon Run. Sockeye salmon spend most of their adult lives at sea, but when they are ready to breed, they travel thousands of miles across the ocean and up rivers, returning to the mountain streams where they were born. Here, they lay their eggs before they die, completing a great circle of life.

However, travelling upstream – against the current – is no easy task. Showing the endurance and strength of a creature many times its size, a salmon can propel itself out of the riverbed and upwards – over rocks, raging rapids... and hungry bears! And if that weren't enough of a challenge, the salmon must also avoid birds such as bald eagles, gulls and ravens, who flock to the river to snatch an easy meal.

GOING NORTH WITH THE
NARWHALS, CANADA

One of nature's most elusive animals, the narwhal, makes an extraordinary journey through narrow passages in the Arctic ice sheet each spring. Revered as the unicorn of the sea because of the male's hornlike tusk, this whale begins its journey in its winter home on the west coast of Greenland. From here, pods of narwhals travel hundreds of kilometres north – dipping and weaving through cracks in the sea ice – to reach bays and fjords filled with fish.

The route is dangerous because the ice is shifting and the cracks could close up at any moment, suffocating the narwhals. But the rewards will be great, so these mysterious mammals persevere. En route, young calves stay close to their mothers, who keep a careful watch for hunters such as orcas and polar bears.

Narwhals spend their lives in the Arctic waters of Canada, Greenland and Russia.

Unlike many other whales, narwhals don't have a dorsal fin. This gives them a smooth shape that allows them to glide under the ice.

The male's horn is actually a tooth that grows in a spiral shape through the upper lip.

It can measure up to 3 metres long!

The narwhal can dive 1,800 metres deep to feed on halibut.

In the Middle Ages, narwhal tusks were sold by hunters as unicorn horns for 10 times their weight in gold!

Baby narwhals are nursed by their mothers for about 20 months – just long enough to learn the skills they need to survive.

Narwhals can grow up to 5 metres long and live for 50 years!

Blowhole

Spiral tusk

Curved tail fluke is used to propel the narwhal along

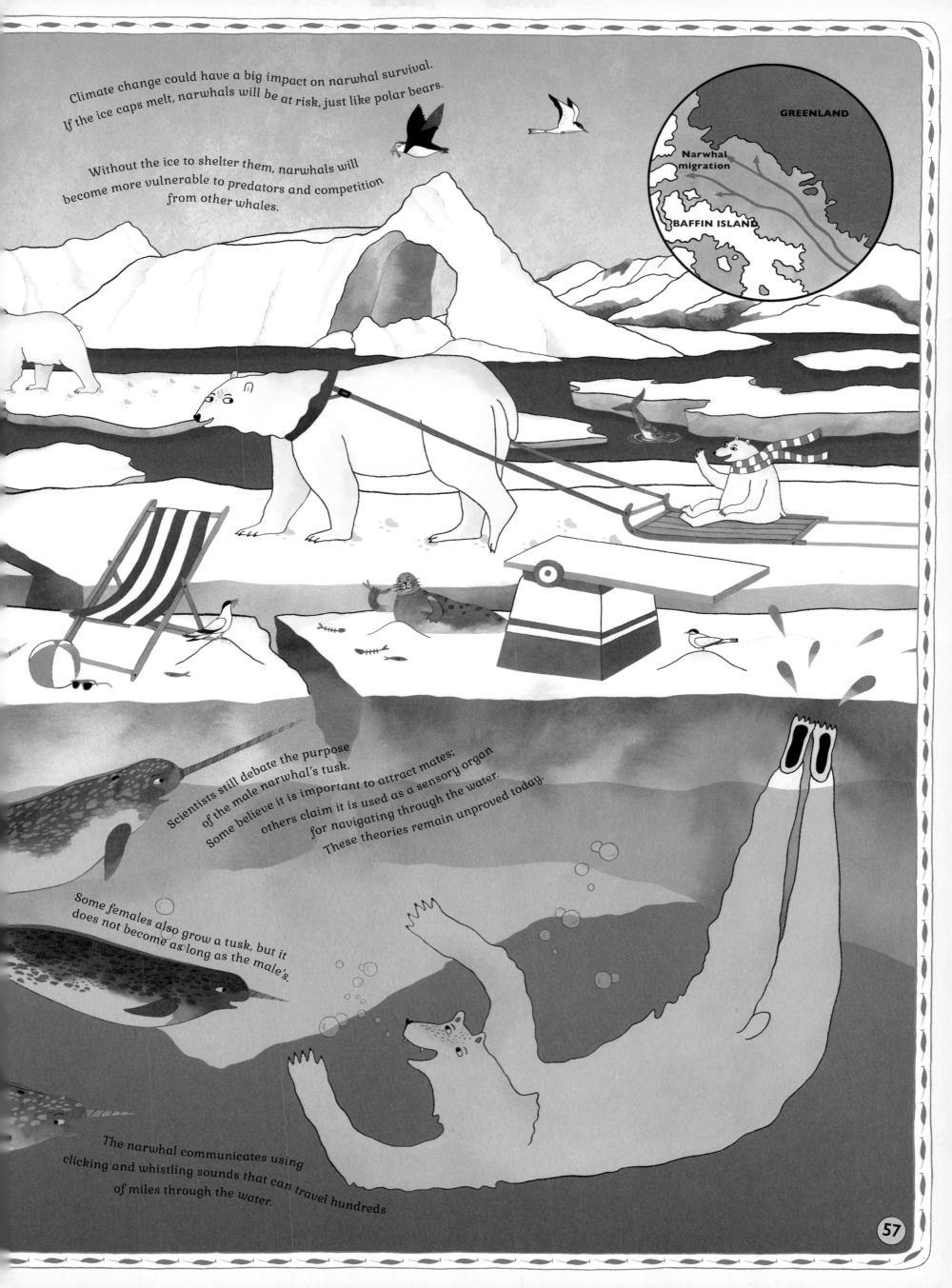

Climate change could have a big impact on narwhal survival. If the ice caps melt, narwhals will be at risk, just like polar bears.

Without the ice to shelter them, narwhals will become more vulnerable to predators and competition from other whales.

GREENLAND

Narwhal migration

BAFFIN ISLAND

Scientists still debate the purpose of the male narwhal's tusk. Some believe it is important to attract mates; others claim it is used as a sensory organ for navigating through the water. These theories remain unproved today.

Some females also grow a tusk, but it does not become as long as the male's.

The narwhal communicates using clicking and whistling sounds that can travel hundreds of miles through the water.

57

Wolves run straight at the herd to cause panic so they can split off the young calves.

Golden eagles have been known to kill young caribou calves.

Unlike other deer species, both male and female caribou have antlers.

Each year, about 3 million caribou migrate across the Arctic tundra.

The females give birth to their calves within a few days of each other. This coordination increases the chances of an individual calf surviving because it is less likely to be taken by predators.

Male antlers are larger than female antlers

Summer coat is short and brown; winter coat is thick and grey

Hoof is hollowed out like a scoop so caribou can dig through snow to find food

Toes spread out in snow to stop caribou from sinking

At top speed, caribou can run at speeds of 80 kilometres per hour!

CANADA

Caribou habitat

A calf and its mother form a strong bond. They recognise each other using scent and sound.

The herds often have to cross icy rivers, which are especially dangerous for the youngsters.

Newborn calves learn to run within hours of being born. At only one day old, a caribou calf can outrun a human!

Life is tough for the caribou calves: about a quarter of them won't survive their first month.

HERDING WITH THE
CARIBOU, CANADA

Caribou herds are always on the move, some travelling more than 3,000 kilometres in a single year! Every spring, the caribou of North America embark on a treacherous journey north to the grazing meadows of the Arctic tundra. In the course of 10 weeks, they may travel 700 kilometres across hazardous landscapes. As the days lengthen, the pregnant females of the herd feel an unmistakable wanderlust: they know it is time to begin their journey north to reach richer pastures before their calves are born. These females lead the migration, with the males following later. It is one of the longest overland journeys of any species on Earth, and it brings many dangers. Wolf packs shadow the herd, eager to seize a chance to pick off the stragglers. Also on the lookout for a meal are hungry bears and opportunistic golden eagles. The caribou must stick together to survive.

UNITED STATES

Great Smoky Mountains

Black bears are found only in North America.

The hands of a black bear are very skilful—as well as being useful for climbing, they can open door latches and even screw-top jars!

Black bears are omnivores, which means they eat all sorts of food, from nuts, berries and leaves to birds, bugs and fish.

Young bears spend lots of time having fun—rolling around, play fighting and swinging on bendy branches.

CLIMBING TREES WITH THE

BLACK BEARS, USA

The Great Smoky Mountains lie in the southeastern United States. They are named after the blue mist that often hangs over their peaks, and they have some very famous inhabitants... black bears! In the spring, a mother bear and her young cubs climb out of their winter den after a long hibernation. The cubs are playful, keen to explore the forest. There aren't many creatures that prey on full-grown bears, but the youngsters may be in danger from bobcats, coyotes and wolves. They can't run very far or fast, but they do have a clever way of getting to safety: climbing. One of the very first skills they learn is how to clamber up a tree. A mother bear often chooses a large white pine as a babysitter for her family! The bark is strong and rough, perfect for clinging to, so the cubs can stay out of harm's way while the mother goes off to find food nearby. After a bit of practise, black bear cubs can easily scramble 30 metres up a tree – then it's time for them to kick back, relax and wait for Mum to return!

Large brain compared to body size; very intelligent

Hearing is twice as sensitive as a human's

Tightly curved claws help bear climb trees

Sense of smell is seven times greater than a bloodhound's

Bears are very strong — they can flip over rocks to find insects to eat. One of their favourite snacks is ant larvae: full of protein!

Bear cubs stay with their mother until they are 18 months old. She teaches them everything they need to know to survive.

Black bears are thought to have the best sense of smell on Earth. They can smell a food source from several miles away.

In the colder months, black bears hibernate. They can survive for seven months without eating or drinking!

A mother communicates with her cubs using grunting sounds. In this way, she lets them know when it is safe to climb down from a tree.

Startling predators
with the
RED-EYED TREE FROG
(Belize)

Coral cruising
with the
CANDY BASSLETS
(Bahamas)

Mexico

Cuba

Bahamas

Belize

Honduras

Guatemala

Jamaica   Haiti   **Dominican Republic**

Nicaragua

St Kitts
& Nevis

Antigua
& Barbuda

**Caribbean
Sea**

Saint
Vincent and the
Grenadines

Dominica

Saint Lucia

El Salvador

Costa Rica

Slow and steady
with the SLOTHS
(Venezuela)

Barbados

Grenada

Trinidad & Tobago

Aerial acrobatics
with the
HUMMINGBIRDS
(Costa Rica)

Panama

Fluttering with
the BLUE MORPHOS
(Panama)

Venezuela

Colombia

Having lunch
with the
GREEN ANACONDA
(Brazil)

Guyana   Suriname French
                    Guia

Posing with the
IGUANAS
(Galápagos Islands)

Ecuador

Prowling with
the JAGUAR
(Guyana)

Scaling dizzy heights
with the LLAMAS (Peru)

Peru

Fungus farming
with the LEAF-
CUTTER ANTS
(Bolivia)

Terrorising termites with the
GIANT ARMADILLO (Brazil)

Bolivia

Paraguay

**South
Pacific
Ocean**

Making some
noise with the
HOWLER MONKEYS
(Argentina)

Argentina

Uruguay

Journeying south
with the
HUMPBACKS (Chile)

Chile

Taking the plunge with the
CAPYBARAS (Argentina)

Dodging
ORCAS
with the
SEA LIONS
(Argentina)

Rock-hopping with the
MAGELLANIC PENGUINS (Argentina)

Falkland Islands

CENTRAL & SOUTH AMERICA

The Amazon is the world's largest rainforest, housing about 30 percent of the Earth's animal and plant species! But South America is not just about the jungle – it is also home to the Galápagos Islands, the Andes Mountains and the remote, wild landscapes of Patagonia, making it a paradise for wildlife lovers!

Squawking with the
GREEN-WINGED MACAWS
(Brazil)

Brazil

Sniffing out a
treat with the
GIANT ANTEATERS
(Brazil)

Piggyback rides with the
GOLDEN LION TAMARINS
(Brazil)

Throwing fruit
with the TOCO
TOUCANS
(Brazil)

South
Atlantic
Ocean

AERIAL ACROBATICS WITH THE
HUMMINGBIRDS, COSTA RICA

In the forests of Costa Rica, you can find some of the world's most impressive aerial acrobats. Over 50 species of hummingbird live here, and they all perform astonishing flying feats. These are among the fastest creatures on Earth: they can fly at 50 kilometres per hour, and can reach nearly 100 kilometres per hour in a dive. They are the stunt pilots of the animal kingdom, flying not only forwards, but also sideways, backwards and even upside down! And they flap their wings at an incredible speed, sometimes 80 times per second, which is faster than the human eye can see. Pulling off exploits like this requires lots of energy. To feed, hummingbirds hover next to flowers, using their sword-shaped bills to probe inside, slurping up nectar with their sticky tongues. They have to eat more than their own body weight in nectar each day to keep going – which is similar to a human eating a whole fridge full of food! Some visit 2,000 flowers in a single day in their quest for energy. With their dazzling, shimmering feathers and their death-defying antics, these tiny dynamos are the jewelled daredevils of the jungle!

The long-billed hermit's curved beak makes up nearly a third of its entire body length.

Despite its tiny size, the ruby-throated hummingbird makes an incredible journey every year. It flies 800 kilometres over the Gulf of Mexico to spend the winter in the U.S.

A hummingbird can extend its tongue as far beyond its beak as the beak is long – perfect for delving inside flowers.

Large brain compared to other birds

Tongue can lap nectar at 13 licks per second!

Wings move in a figure-of-eight pattern for speed and agility

Hollow bones keep the bird light

An average human takes about 20 breaths per minute; a hummingbird takes 250!

The scintillant hummingbird is the smallest in Costa Rica, weighing just over 2 grams. By contrast, a 20p coin weighs 5 grams!

COSTA RICA

Hummingbird habitat

The bronzy hermit hummingbird collects cobwebs, then weaves the silk into a cradle hung from a leaf to protect her youngsters.

Some hummingbirds are so small that they can get trapped in spiders' webs!

Hummingbirds have amazing memories: they can remember where every flower in their territory is, and they know how long each one takes to refill with nectar!

A hummingbird's feet are so tiny that the bird can't actually walk on the ground; the feet are just used for perching.

At night, flower petals close up, so a hummingbird has to save energy: its heart rate and body temperature plummet as it enters a mini hibernation.

The Galápagos hawk is a fearsome predator of young iguanas, attacking them with its hooked talons.

Galápagos Islands

SOUTH AMERICA

Iguanas are cold-blooded, which means they take on the temperature of their surroundings. They bask in the sun to warm up, spreading themselves out to soak up maximum rays.

Most female iguanas do not swim because their small bodies lose heat too quickly in the cold water.

Scientists think that marine iguanas may be descended from land iguanas that floated out to the islands on rafts of vegetation millions of years ago.

Marine iguanas take in a lot of salt because they eat so much seaweed. To get rid of this salt, they sneeze it out. The salt sometimes lands on their heads, making a white wig!

Males can measure up to 1.5 metres long

Blunt nose and sharp teeth help iguana scrape seaweed off rocks

Iguana moves its long, flat tail from side to side to swim

Huge claws grip rocks while iguana is feeding

IGUANAS, GALÁPAGOS ISLANDS

The Galápagos Islands lie 1000 kilometres away from the coast of South America, in the Pacific. This remote group of volcanic islands is home to a surprising collection of wildlife. Some of the Galápagos's most famous inhabitants are its marine iguanas. These scaly sunbathers live on land but feed in the sea – they are the only sea-going lizards on the planet!

In the breeding season, the iguanas of Española Island do their best to impress the ladies. The males, who are usually a dull black colour, go through a dramatic transformation, turning bright shades of red and green. But it's not just about looking the part: if he is to win a mate, a male iguana must act the tough guy too. At this time of year, males will often fight each other, pushing, shoving and headbutting to prove their strength. It makes for quite a show!

Marine iguanas feed on seaweed. Their strong claws allow them to hold on to rocks while feeding so they don't get washed away.

Large male iguanas dive into the water to reach the best seaweed. They have to return to land to warm up again after about 10 minutes.

When food is scarce, marine iguanas don't just become thinner – they actually shrink in length too.

A territorial fight between two male iguanas can last for up to five hours!

The iguanas may get their red and green colouring from eating certain types of seaweed during the breeding season.

A single ant can carry a piece of leaf up to 50 times its own body weight!

Some species of leaf-cutter ant can strip a whole tree bare of leaves in a single night.

Guard ants may ride on top of the leaves carried by foragers, to fend off attacks from parasitic flies.

Once a soldier ant's jaws have clamped shut, they stay closed, even if its body gets ripped off!

Rubbish-collector ants work hard to keep the colony clean, carrying any waste to dumps deep underground.

Humans have been farming crops for thousands of years; leaf-cutter ants have been farming fungus for millions of years!

Worker ants groom, clean and feed the queen.

The queen is the size of a small mouse—huge compared to the other ants.

The queen's role is to lay eggs, which will hatch into future members of the colony. She may lay a million eggs per year.

Types of Leaf-Cutter Ant

Worker ants go out to collect leaves

The queen is the largest of the leaf-cutter ants

Soldier ants protect the workers from predators

The smallest ants, called minims, do jobs inside the colony

Amazon
Rainforest

BOLIVIA

Young leaf-cutters have very sharp jaws, but these wear out as they get older, so older ants often carry leaves cut by others.

Ants communicate using scents: they can find a foraging site 100 metres away by following the scent signals left by their fellow ants.

The underground colony is enormous, reaching a depth of 6 metres, and holding up to 8 million ants! It may have around 1,000 different chambers.

FUNGUS FARMING WITH THE

LEAF-CUTTER ANTS, BOLIVIA

The floor of the Bolivian rainforest is patrolled by an army of incredible insects: leaf-cutter ants. These are the farmers of the insect world. The ants set out in huge processions from their underground colony. They use their strong jaws to cut off pieces of leaf from the surrounding trees, which they carry back to the nest. Then the ants grind the leaves into a compost, which they use to grow a special fungus that feeds the colony.

Each ant has its own job to do: some are cutters, some carriers; some tend the fungus, while others look after the queen. And some of the largest ants are soldiers, whose role is to protect the colony. They have enormous, powerful jaws that lock on to anything, or anyone, that threatens their queen. In fact, their jaws are so powerful that the locals have been known to use them to hold wounds closed, like stitches!

HAVING LUNCH WITH THE
GREEN ANACONDA, BRAZIL

In the shallows of a Brazilian rainforest swamp, all appears calm. Light dapples the surface and a deer comes to drink at the water's edge, but something is lurking in the fading light... A member of the boa family, the anaconda is the largest snake in the world, measuring up to 9 metres – as long as a bus! Cumbersome on land, it is stealthy and sleek in the water, where it waits for passing prey. It pokes its snout above the surface, ready to strike. The anaconda is a constrictor, killing prey by coiling its body around a victim and squeezing until the animal suffocates. This huge snake maintains its size by eating a mighty diet: wild pigs, deer and sometimes even caimans and jaguars. It can unhinge its jaw to swallow prey much wider than itself. After a big meal, the anaconda can go for weeks without food.

In the wild, the green anaconda lives for up to 10 years.

Young anacondas are at risk of being killed by predators such as caimans, which, in turn, are hunted by adult anacondas!

Unlike the majority of snakes, which hatch from eggs, baby anacondas are born live. The female gives birth to up to 40 babies at a time.

Baby anacondas are just over half a metre long when they are born. They instinctively know how to hunt and survive on their own.

Muscular coils suffocate prey

Stomach produces powerful juices that slowly digest food

Green-brown colouring helps snake stay hidden in swamp

Jaws can open wider than width of head and body

Green anaconda habitat

BRAZIL

In spring, males seek female mates. This can result in a breeding ball, where many males wrap themselves around a female.

A coiling anaconda does not crush its victim or even break its bones. It simply stops its prey's breathing, then swallows it whole!

The anaconda's eyes and nostrils are on top of its head so it can look out for prey and breathe while remaining hidden underwater.

Snakes use their forked tongues to 'taste' their surroundings. The tongue collects scents from the air, sending messages to the brain.

This swamp-dweller lives in the marshes and slow-moving streams of the South American rainforest.

The record-breaking anaconda can weigh over 200 kilograms: about as much as seven 10-year-olds! The females are much larger than the males.

A humpback's tail fin is like a giant fingerprint: the black-and-white markings are unique, which means that scientists can tell the whales apart.

The eerie 'song' of a humpback whale is a collection of moans, sighs and roars that can travel hundreds of kilometres underwater. Scientists think that the whale makes these sounds to attract mates.

Measuring up to 5 metres in length, the flipper of a humpback whale is the longest appendage of any animal on Earth!

The heart of a humpback weighs nearly 200 kilograms, as much as three adult men.

Although humpbacks must come to the surface to breathe, they can hold their breath underwater for up to 45 minutes.

JOURNEYING SOUTH WITH THE

HUMPBACKS, CHILE

Whales are some of the most amazing animals on the planet. Not only are they the world's largest creatures, but they also undertake incredibly long journeys. Oceans have no walls, fences, roads or railways to cross, so it's easier for wildlife to travel huge distances than on land. And the humpback whale holds the record for the longest migration of any mammal, sometimes travelling more than 16,000 kilometres per year: nearly half the distance round the globe! As winter approaches in oceans all over the world, humpback whales migrate towards the equator, where they breed. Then, each spring, they return to their summer feeding grounds near the poles. Chile has over 4,000 kilometres of coastline, so its waters often host these mighty creatures as they make their lengthy journeys. Along the way, they perform impressive feats of acrobatics, often leaping almost clear of the water. Some humpbacks have been seen doing this 80 times in a row, which is astonishing, especially when you remember that they weigh about the same as 400 people!

Why do humpbacks leap from the water? It might be because the noise they make when they land sends messages to other whales; it might be to clean their skin; or it might be just for fun!

Humpback Migration Routes

CHILE

A humpback feeds on tiny creatures called krill. It opens its mouth and scoops in water, then forces the water out through a sievelike plate at the front of its mouth, leaving the krill behind.

Humpback whales often migrate in small groups, called pods. Mothers and calves travel together, sometimes touching each other with their flippers.

In 2010, a lone female humpback travelled more than 9,800 kilometres from Brazil to Madagascar in the longest mammal migration ever recorded.

Humpback calves don't stop growing until they are 10 years old! A full-grown whale can measure up to 19 metres long.

Two blowholes fire water up to 15 feet into the air

Huge tail fin helps propel whale

Sievelike filter at front of mouth

Knobbly bumps called tubercles help whale sense movements in the water

DODGING ORCAS WITH THE

SEA LIONS, ARGENTINA

The Valdes Peninsula in southern Argentina is a haven for wildlife, home to thousands of sea lions, elephant seals and penguins. Each March, just after the sea lion pups are born, the beaches here become the setting for one of nature's most unusual events. As the youngsters cluster together at the water's edge, they may appear to be safe, but danger is never far away...

Every year, the same group of orcas patrols these shores, awaiting the birth of the pups. They use channels of deep water to get close to the beach, then hurl themselves ashore to snatch up sea lions. These orcas are very daring: no other whale beaches itself in this way. This feeding frenzy takes place for only a couple of weeks each year; before long, the sea lions learn to stay away from the water's edge!

Orcas often carry the sea lions back to the deeper water before killing them. They sometimes throw the pups around, as if playing with them.

The largest orca ever measured was 9.8 metres long, which is nearly as long as a double-decker bus!

To grab prey, orcas use their huge teeth, which can grow up to 10 centimetres long.

A killer whale needs to eat the equivalent of three sea lion pups a day to get all the energy it needs.

The pups make their first trips into the water at about four weeks old – this is when they are most likely to be attacked. By two months old, they are much stronger swimmers.

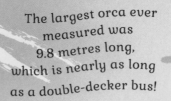

Each time an orca flings itself onto the beach, it risks getting stuck; it must thrash violently to get back into the water.

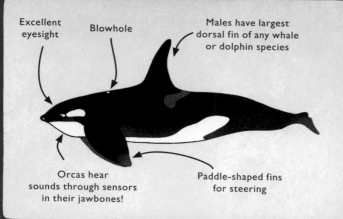

Excellent eyesight

Blowhole

Males have largest dorsal fin of any whale or dolphin species

Orcas hear sounds through sensors in their jawbones!

Paddle-shaped fins for steering

How do you tell the difference between a seal and a sea lion? Look at the ears! A sea lion has a small ear flap on each side of its head, while seals just have tiny holes.

Fully grown male sea lions are about three times the size of females! An adult male has a massive head and neck, with thick fur that looks like a lion's mane.

The Valdes Peninsula is home to the largest colony of Magellanic penguins in the world.

Sea lion mothers stay with their pups for a week after birth. Then they head off to hunt at sea, leaving the youngsters on the beach — easy pickings for a passing orca!

ARGENTINA

Valdes Peninsula

South Orkney Islands

Gliding with the
ALBATROSS
(South Shetland Islands)

South Shetland Islands

Southern Ocean

Journeying south with the
BLUE WHALE (Weddell Sea)

Weddell Sea

Flying long-haul
with the
ARCTIC TERNS
(Weddell Sea)

Battling the Antarctic
toothfish with the
COLOSSAL SQUID
(Bellingshausen Sea)

Antarctica

Ronne Ice Shelf

Bellingshausen Sea

Amundsen
Sea

Ross Ice Shelf

Trailing tentacles with the
COMB JELLYFISH
(Amundsen Sea)

Ross Sea

Deep-diving with the
WEDDELL SEALS (Ross Sea)

South Pacific
Ocean

ANTARCTICA

At the end of the Earth, covered in ice, lies Antarctica: the coldest, windiest and driest continent in the world. To withstand the freezing conditions, wildlife here must be tough and resourceful. Prepare to meet some of the hardiest survivors on the planet!

Guarding the nest with the SNOW PETRELS (Queen Maud Land)

On the hunt with the LEOPARD SEAL (Amery Ice Shelf)

Amery Ice Shelf

Huddling with the EMPEROR PENGUINS (Shackleton Ice Shelf)

Indian Ocean

Waddling ashore with the ADÉLIE PENGUINS (Adélie Coast)

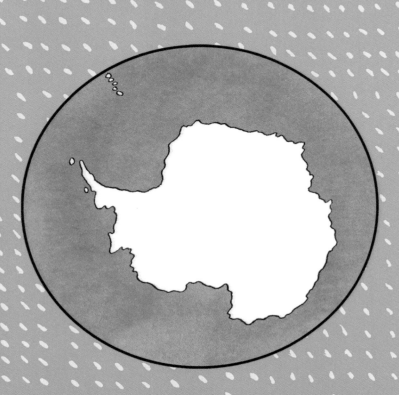

Tasman Sea

Trunk tussles with the ELEPHANT SEAL (Victoria Land)

Arctic terns don't migrate in large flocks, but they all make their journeys at similar times, coming together to feed on krill in the Weddell Sea of Antarctica.

On their journey south, the terns make a long stop in the North Atlantic, where the waters are rich in fish to eat. They fuel up here for their long journey.

Terns use the winds to fly long distances: their journey north usually takes half the time of the trip south because they hitch a lift on the wind currents.

The wandering albatross is another record-breaking bird found in the Antarctic: its outstretched wings measure up to 3.5 metres, giving it the largest wingspan of any bird!

The Arctic tern spends most of its time in the air and rarely lands – it hunts, eats and even sleeps on the wing!

These globetrotters nest in the Arctic. During the summer there, there are 24 hours of daylight, which means more time to collect food for the chicks.

An Arctic tern can live for over 30 years!

Long, forked tail and long wings make tern an excellent flier

Dark wing tips

Black cap

Hollow bones keep bird light

Pointed red beak for catching food

FLYING LONG-HAUL WITH THE
ARCTIC TERNS, WEDDELL SEA

The Arctic tern is a small bird weighing about the same as a lemon. But despite its little size, this bird has a large claim to fame: it makes the longest migration of any animal on Earth. In a single year, it can cover a colossal 70,000 kilometres from pole to pole and back again. This means that in its lifetime, an Arctic tern may have travelled the same distance as flying to the moon and back three times! At the end of each summer, the bird sets out from the Arctic, heading south all the way across the globe towards Antarctica. It will spend about four months here before taking flight again and travelling back to the Arctic. So why does the bird make this epic journey? This migration means that the Arctic tern always has plentiful food to eat, and never has to live through a full-blown winter: when it's winter in the south, the tern is in the north, and vice versa. The Arctic tern sees more daylight than any other creature – in fact, for eight months each year, the sun never sets on it!

The birds catch fish and other sea creatures by swooping down from above and seizing prey from the water's surface.

The southern giant petrel also lives in the Antarctic, using its huge beak to tear into whale, seal and penguin carcasses.

The snow petrel is a pure-white Antarctic bird that has been found as far south as the South Pole!

Tern migration routes

Weddell Sea

79

HUDDLING WITH THE
EMPEROR PENGUINS, SHACKLETON ICE SHELF

Welcome to the coldest place on Earth. July finds the Antarctic in winter's grip, with average temperatures falling to -30° Celsius, and blizzards gusting at over 160 kilometres per hour. Yet here on the ice, hundreds of emperor penguins are gathering. These are the biggest penguins in the world, with each male measuring over a metre tall. It is the males' job to keep the eggs warm while the females are feeding at sea. Each male balances an egg on his feet, tucked safely under a fold of skin. These penguins have amazing stamina to survive the Antarctic's freezing storms. To keep out the cold, they cluster in a tight huddle of up to 6,000. The group is a shuffling mass, as the penguins constantly manoeuvre themselves towards the warm centre. *Brrrrr!*

Between March and May, the penguins gather on the sea ice to breed. They can travel over 95 kilometres from the sea to reach their breeding site.

In May or June, each female penguin lays a single egg, which the male balances on his feet, tucking it under a fold of skin to keep warm.

The female leaves the male with the egg while she returns to the sea to feed — eating at least 2 kilograms of fish per day.

The males huddle for nearly 4 months to keep their eggs warm. During this time, they do not feed and will lose nearly half their body weight!

Each male on the outside of the huddle shuffles towards the inside so everyone gets a chance to stay warm.

Emperor penguin habitat

ANTARCTICA

Shackleton Ice Shelf

The chicks hatch in August, and the mother returns to feed her baby with regurgitated fish.

Once back, the mother guards the chick while the father feeds at sea. When he returns, both parents take turns looking after the chick.

At about 6 weeks old, the chicks gather in crèches for warmth, allowing the parents to go and hunt.

In water, the penguin's black back blends in with the dark ocean floor, making it hard to see the penguin from above

By December, the youngsters are ready to go to sea and look after themselves, but they must be on the lookout for orcas and leopard seals!

Penguin can't fly but uses wings as paddles for swimming

White stomach blends in with the bright sky, making it hard to see penguin from below

DEEP-DIVING WITH THE

WEDDELL SEALS, ROSS SEA

You would think that nothing could survive in the frozen Antarctic waters, but the Weddell seal thrives here. It is one of the toughest mammals on Earth, able to live all year in these bitter temperatures. The seal must work for its meals, diving deep into the dark waters to catch fish. It is well equipped for the job: it can dive more than 700 metres, which is eight times the height of Big Ben! And it can stay underwater for over 45 minutes. If you were to dive this deep, the pressure would crush you, so how does the seal manage? It can fold down its ribcage and collapse its lungs to avoid them being damaged during a dive. It can also store oxygen in its body tissues – like having an inbuilt scuba tank!

The seals must come to the surface to breathe through air holes in the ice.

The fierce leopard seal sometimes preys on penguins and Weddell pups, shaking its prey from side to side to kill it.

Before it dives, a Weddell seal takes a few deep breaths to boost its oxygen levels, like charging up a battery...

Then it forces most of the air out of its lungs so that it doesn't float. This way, it can glide downwards through the water.

Weddell seals spend a lot of time below the Antarctic ice – this helps them avoid hunters such as orcas and leopard seals.

Weddell seal habitat

ANTARCTICA

Ross Sea

Weddell seals sometimes sleep at their breathing holes, with their snouts pushed out into the air!

Weddell seals call to each other while underwater. These calls can sometimes be heard above the ice.

To scare fish out of their hidey holes, Weddell seals can blow air into cracks in the ice.

During a deep dive, the Weddell seal's heart rate drops to just four beats per minute! This allows it to save oxygen while underwater.

Another expert diver in these waters is the elephant seal — it can plunge down to 1.5 kilometres and hold its breath for two hours!

Eyes can see well even in bad light

Torpedo-shaped body

Closable ears and nostrils

Strong flippers

Thick layer of blubber for warmth

CAN YOU FIND?

Crocodile, **Kenya**

African rock python, **Zambia**

Gannets, **South Africa**

Yellow-billed kite, **West Africa**

Sea lion, **Greenland**

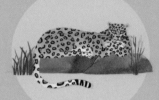
Sri Lankan Leopard, **Sri Lanka**

Mama and Baby Panda, **Panda**

Macaques, **Borneo**

Azure Kingfisher **Australia**

Galah, **Australia**

Scuba-diving bear **Alaska, USA**

Well-fed walrus, **Canada**

Red squirrel **USA**

Galapagos hawk, **Galapagos**

Guard ants, **Germany**

Caiman, **Brazil**

Sloth bear, **Sri Lanka**

Bananas, **Borneo**

Seal building a sandcastle, **Argentina**

Tent, **Weddell Sea**

Spotted deer, **Sri Lanka**

Water rats, **Australia**

Snow-penguin, **Shackleton Ice Shelf**

Weddell seal fishing, **Ross Sea**

Lion, **Kenya**

Hungry crocodile, **Zambia**

Shark, **South Africa**

Crab, **West Africa**

Arctic wolf, **Greenland**

Puffin parachuting, **Iceland**

Queen Bee,
British Isles

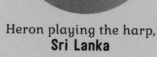

Heron playing the harp,
Sri Lanka

Neesia fruit,
Borneo

Butterfly,
New Guinea

Blue feather,
Australia

Kangaroo wearing
sunglasses, **Australia**

Grizzly bear fishing,
Alaska

Diving board,
Canada

Squirrels having a picnic
USA

Iguana under an
umbrella, **Galapagos**

Coral,
West Africa

Platypus letterbox,
Australia

Parrot,
Brazil

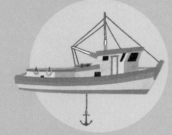

Boat,
Chile

Beach ball,
Argentina

Arctic tern fishing,
Weddell Sea

Stripey deck chair,
Canada

Penguin tobogganing,
Shackleton Ice Shelf

Mother penguin
feeding her baby,
Shackleton Ice Shelf

Penguin throwing a
snowball,
Shackleton Ice Shelf

Baby bowerbird in nest,
New Guinea and Australia

Seal eating ice
cone, **Ross Sea**

Long-billed hermit,
Costa Rica

Raccoon,
USA

Baby narwhal
Canada

Bald Eagle,
Alaska

Sturt's Desert Pea,
Australia

Clouded leopard,
Borneo

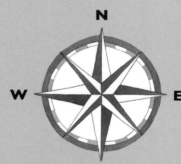

85

INDEX

First published in Great Britain in 2016 by Wide Eyed Editions,
an imprint of Aurum Press, 74–77 White Lion Street, London N1 9PF
QuartoKnows.com
Visit our blogs at QuartoKnows.com
Atlas of Animal Adventures copyright © Aurum Press Ltd 2016
Illustrations copyright © Lucy Letherland 2016

A catalogue record for this book is available from the British Library.

ISBN 978-1-84780-792-2

Illustrated with coloured inks

Set in Festivo, Gabriela and Gill Sans Shadow

Designed by Joe Hales and Andrew Watson
Edited by Emily Hawkins
Published by Rachel Williams

Printed in China

1 3 5 7 9 8 6 4 2

MIX
Paper from
responsible sources
FSC® C104723